Piano Recital Showcase

FESTIVAL FAVORITES

10 OUTSTANDING NFMC SELECTED SOLOS

ISBN 978-1-4803-3778-7

HAL•LEONARD®
CORPORATION
7777 W. BLUEMOUND RD. P.O. BOX 13819 MILWAUKEE, WI 53213

In Australia Contact:
Hal Leonard Australia Pty. Ltd.
4 Lentara Court
Cheltenham, Victoria, 3192 Australia
Email: ausadmin@halleonard.com.au

Visit Hal Leonard Online at
www.halleonard.com

CONTENTS

Barcarolle Impromptu

To David Kaiserman

By Bruce Berr

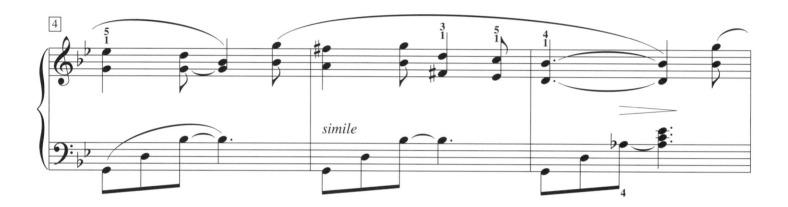

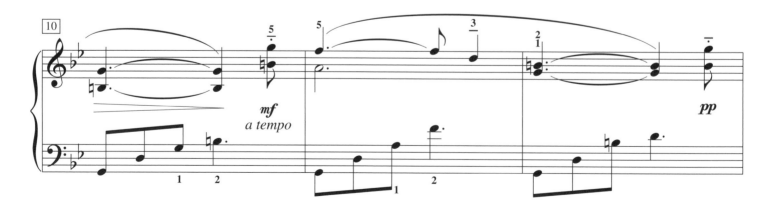

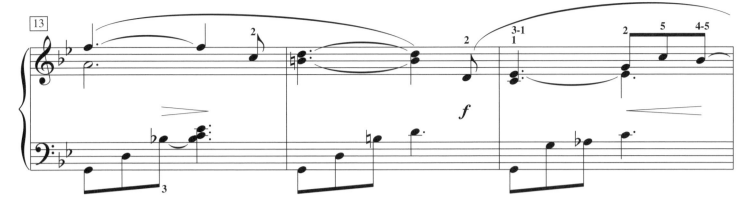

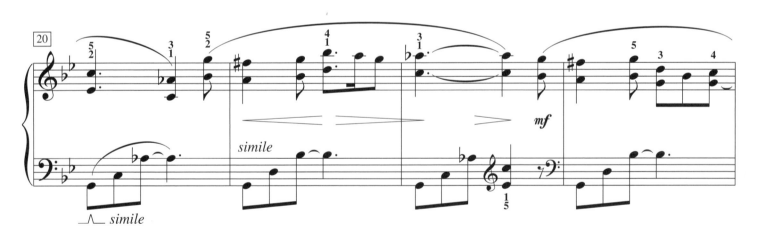

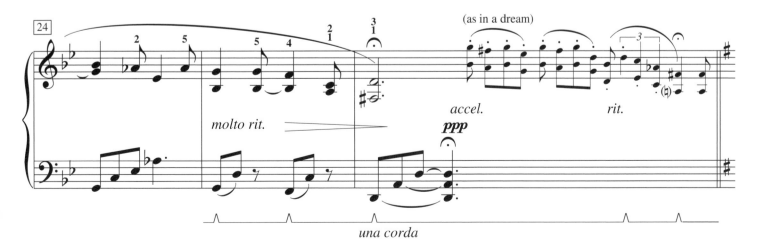

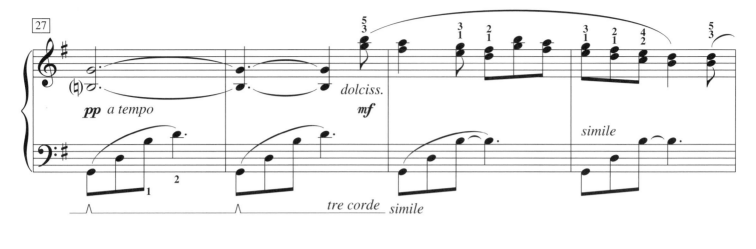

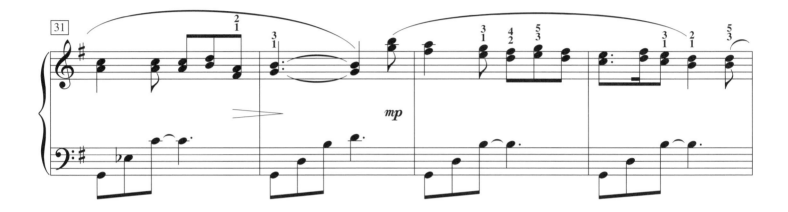

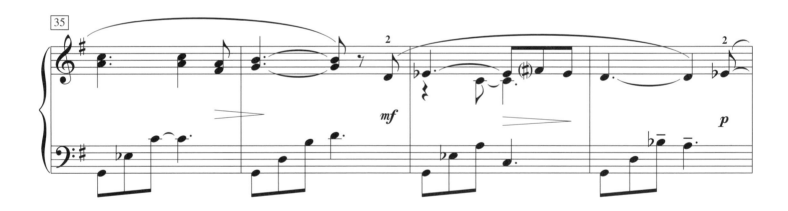

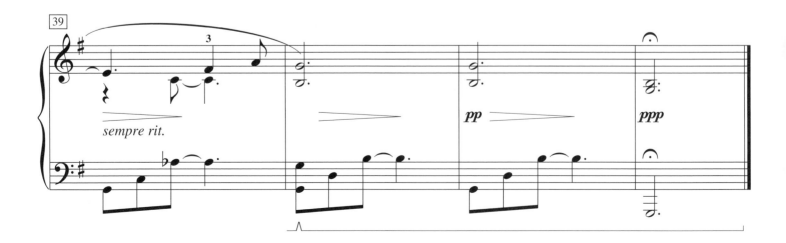

Dance of the Trolls

By Carol Klose

With urgency (♩. = 84)

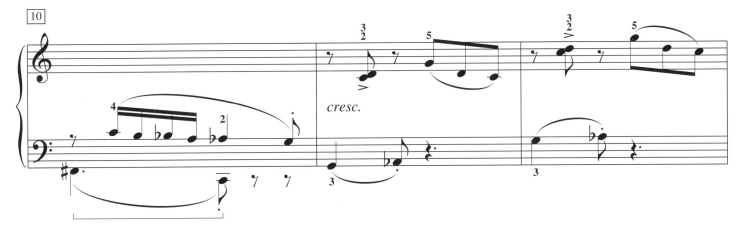

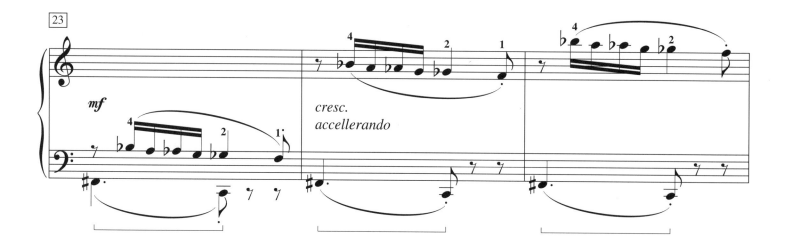

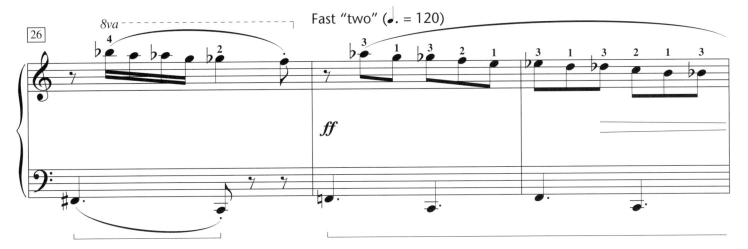

Fast "two" (♩. = 120)

Cathedral Echoes
(Harp Song)

By Mona Rejino

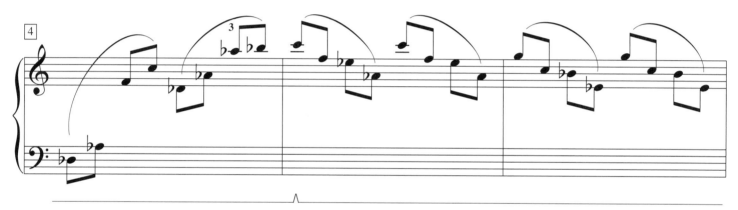

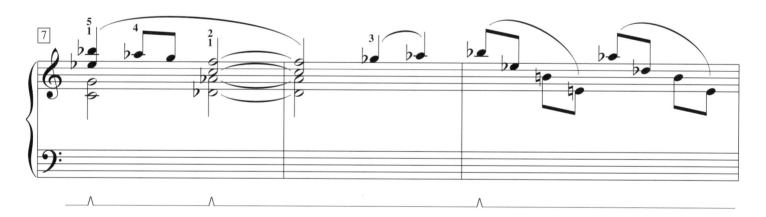

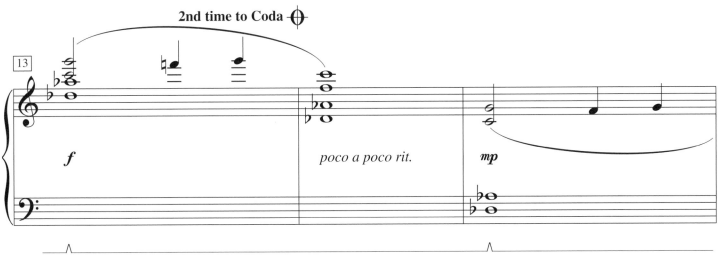

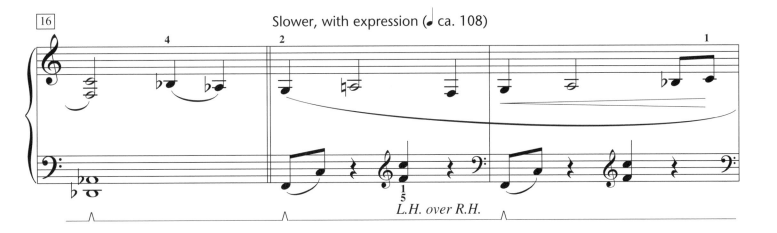

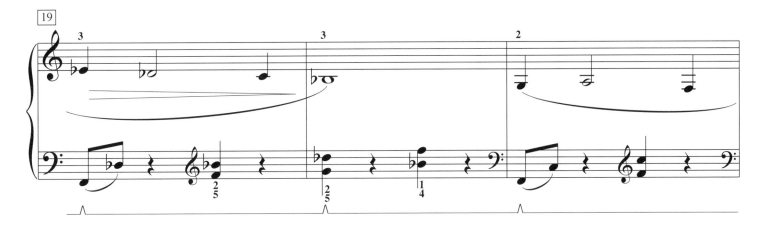

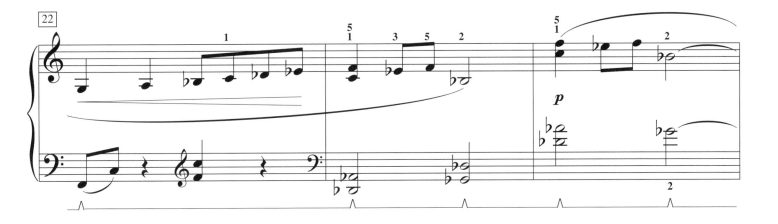

12

Slightly faster (♩ ca. 116)

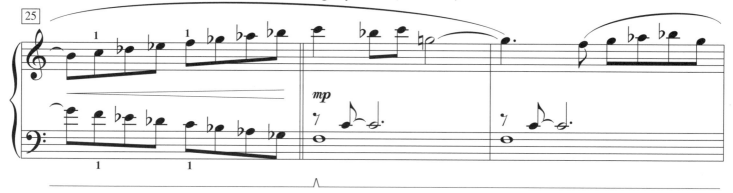

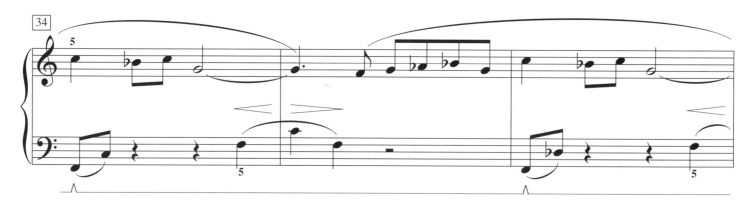

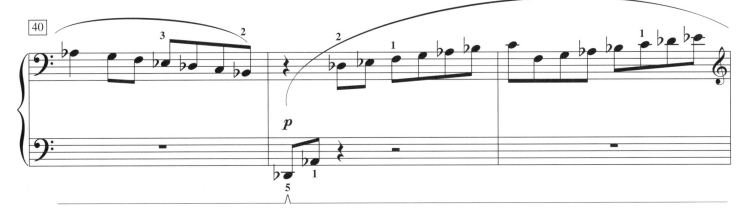

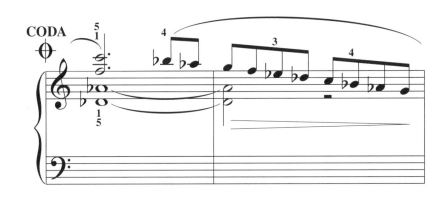

Jasmine in the Mist

for my husband John

By Carol Klose

Moderato (♩=112)

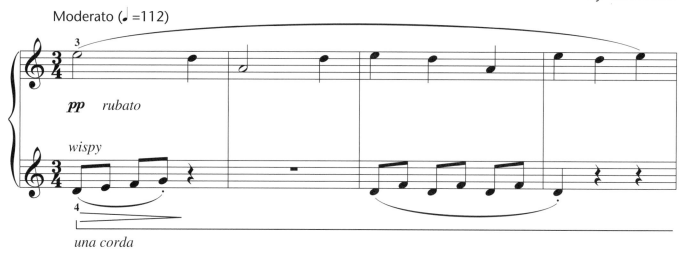

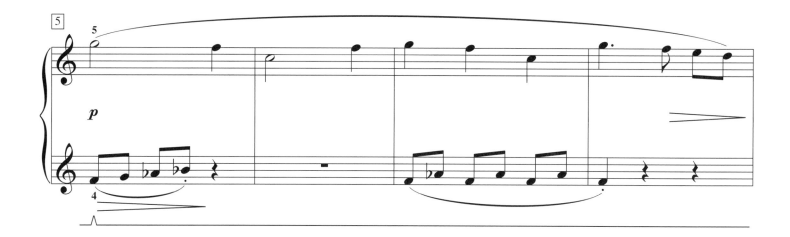

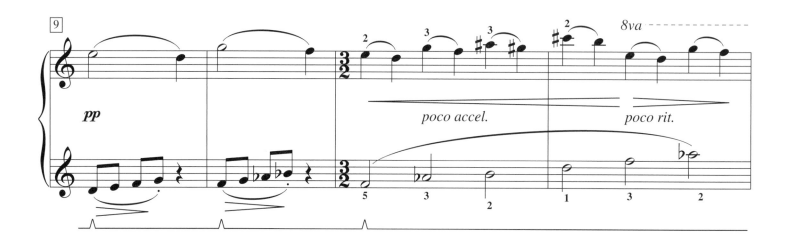

Like misty raindrops (♩ = 120)

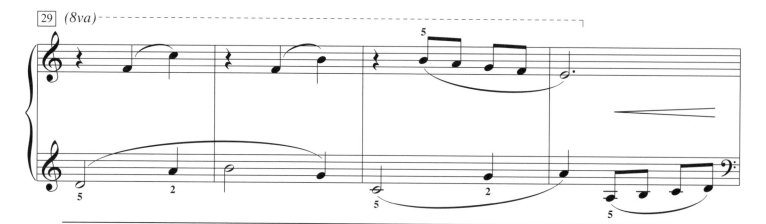

Poco più mosso (♩=126-132)

LH cantabile

tre corde

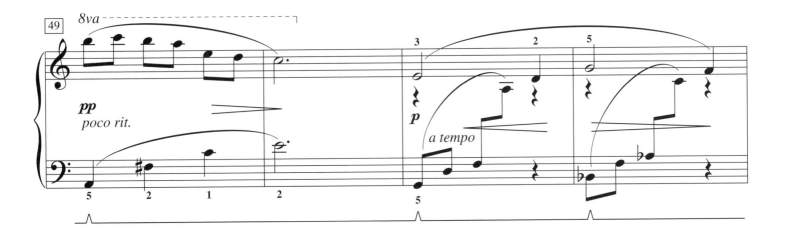

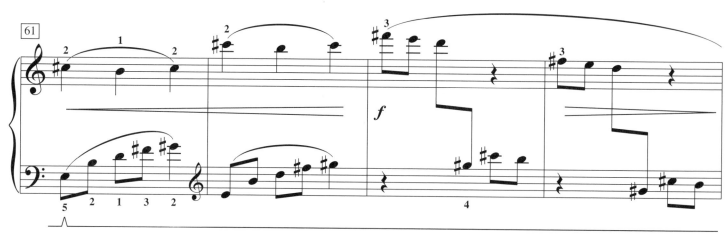

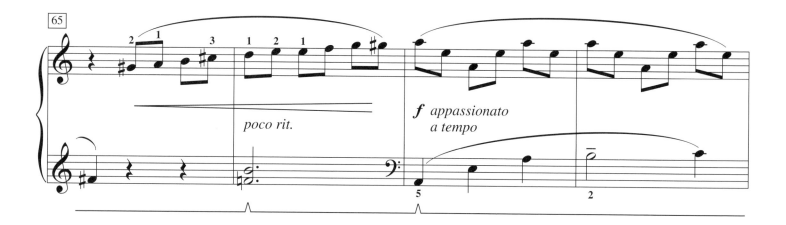

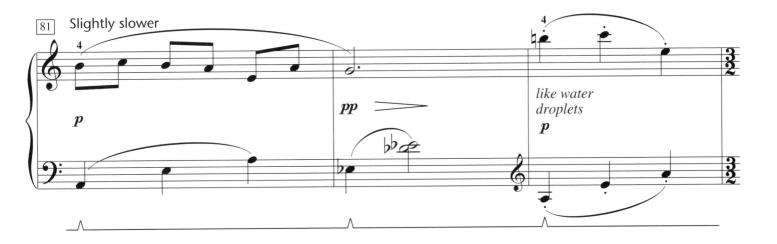

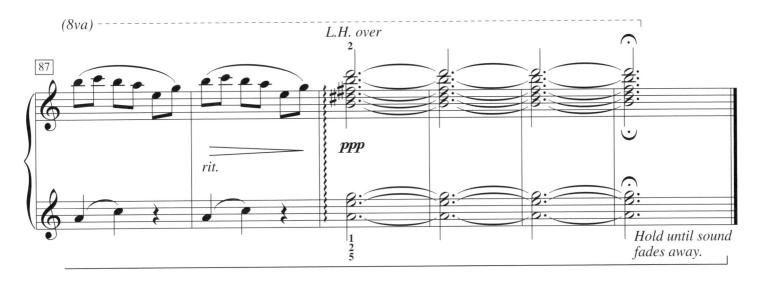

Maestro, There's a Fly in My Waltz

By Carol Klose

Moderate Waltz tempo, with a lilt (= 168)

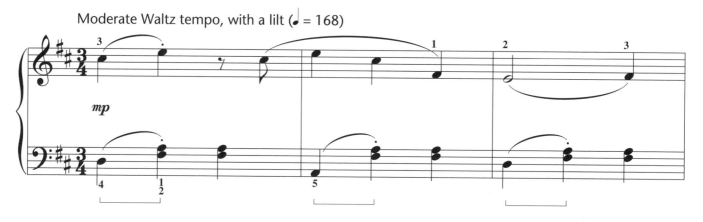

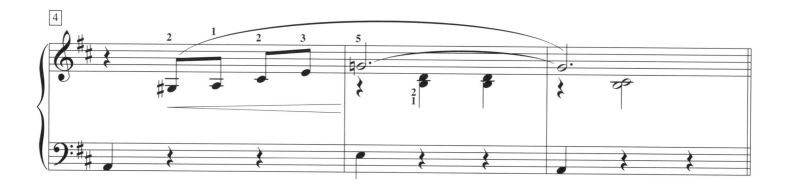

Presto ("Fly" motif)

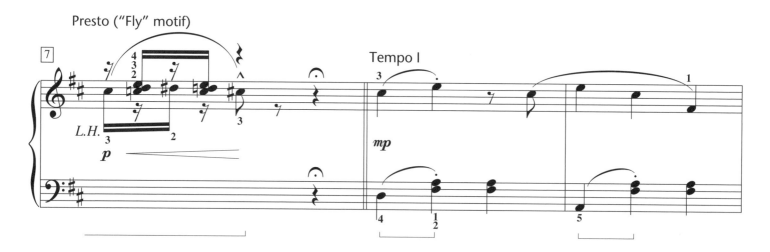

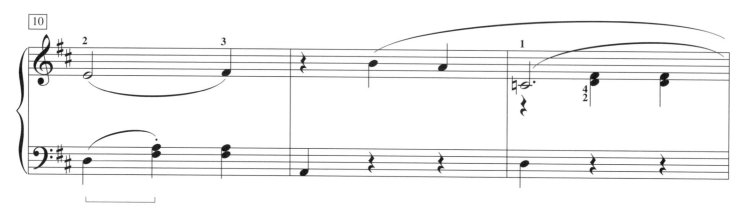

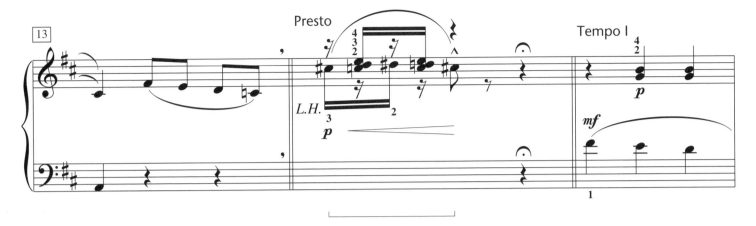

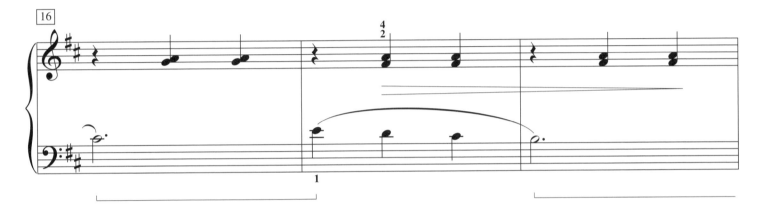

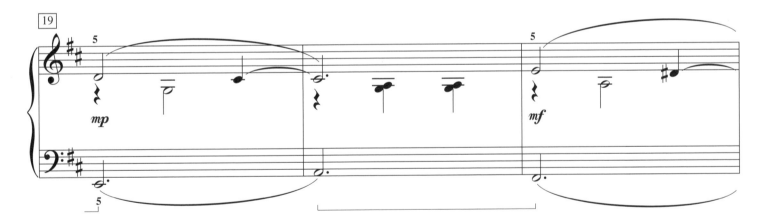

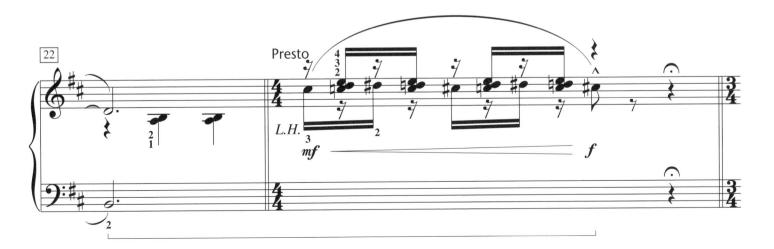

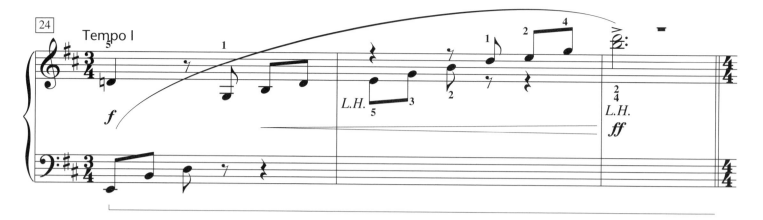

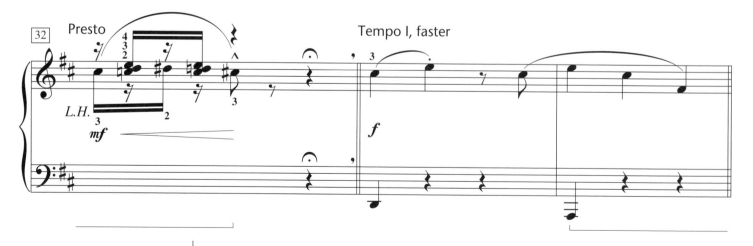

*Glissando for one beat. ✕ = approximate pitch.

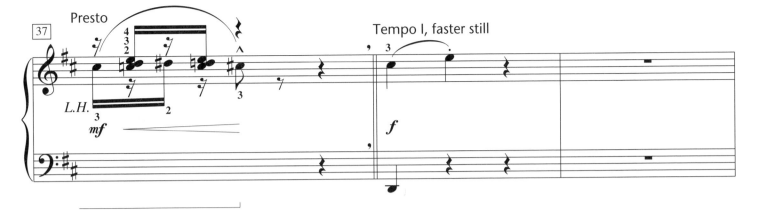

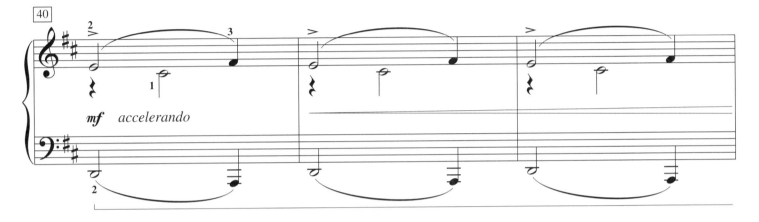

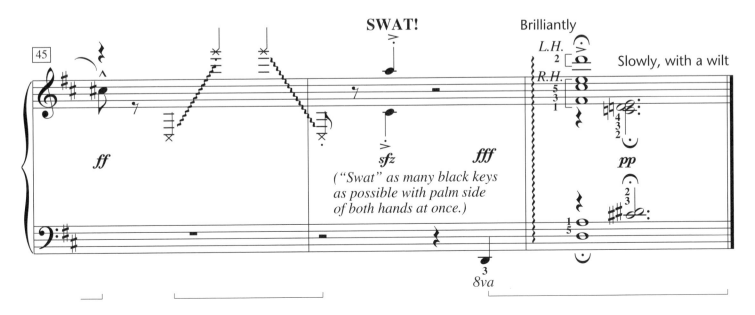

Mother Earth, Sister Moon

By Carol Klose

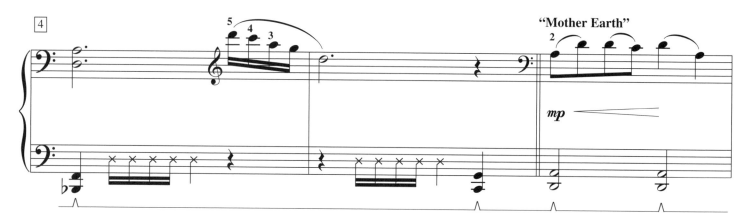

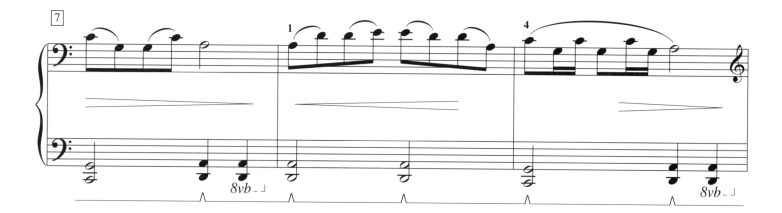

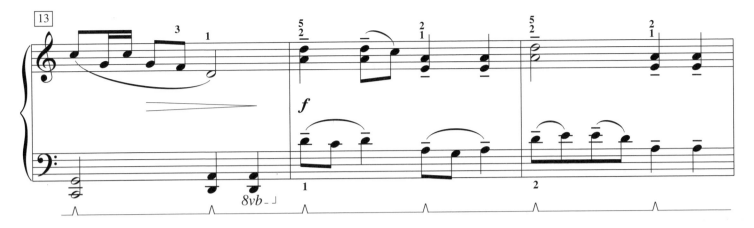

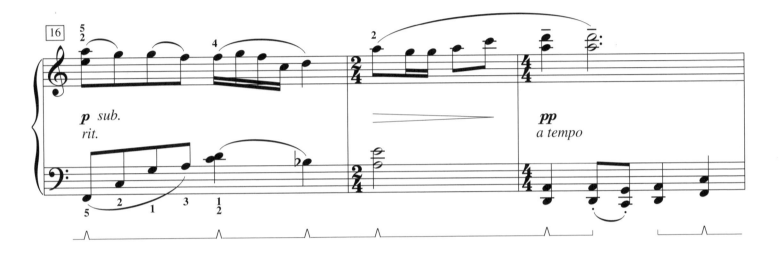

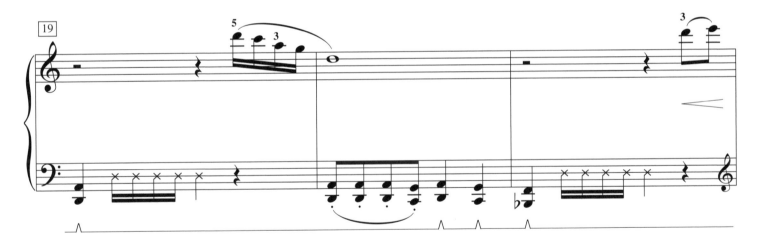

"Sister Moon"

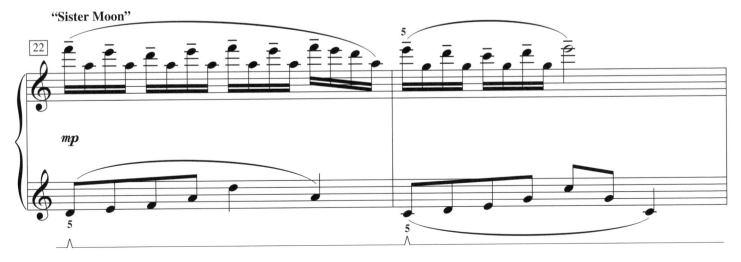

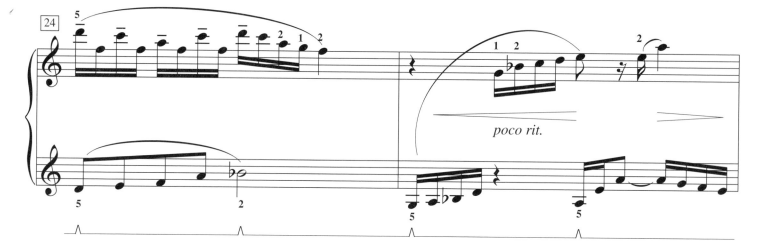

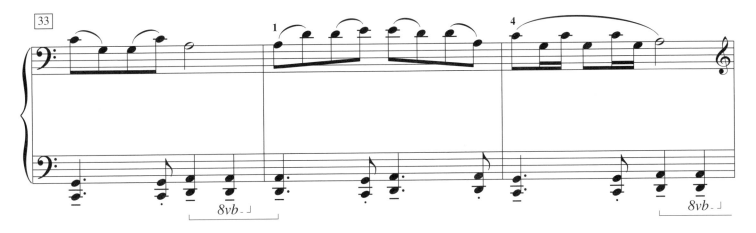

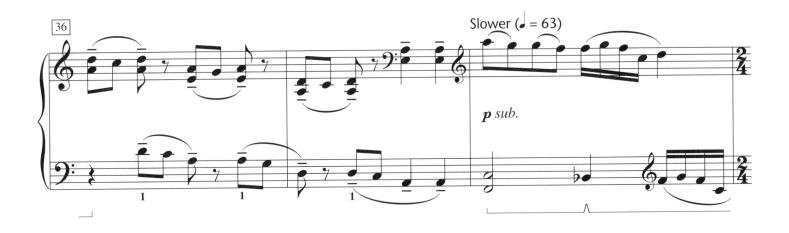

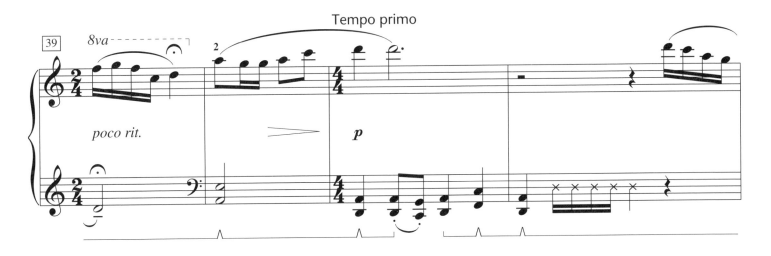

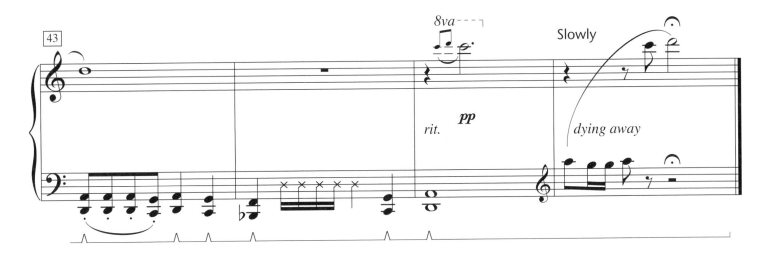

Un phare dans le brouillard

A Lighthouse in the Fog

By Jennifer Linn

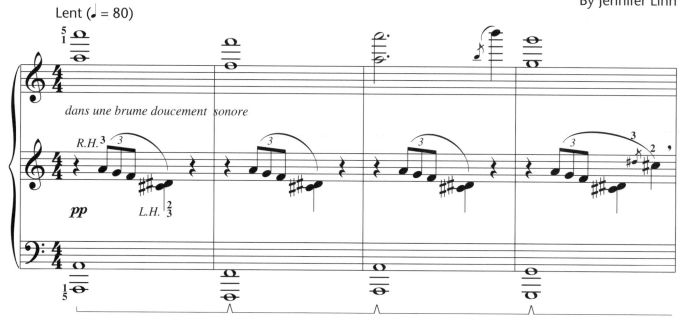

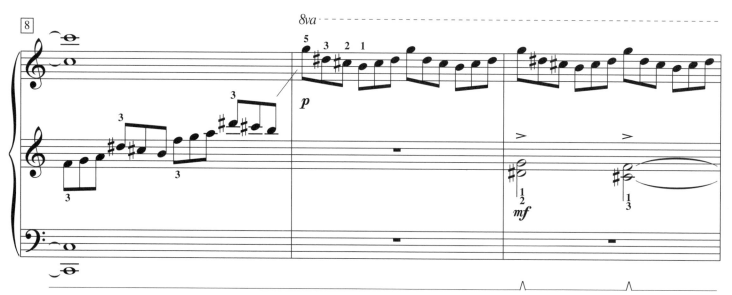

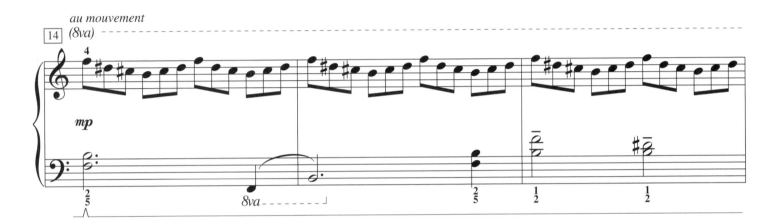

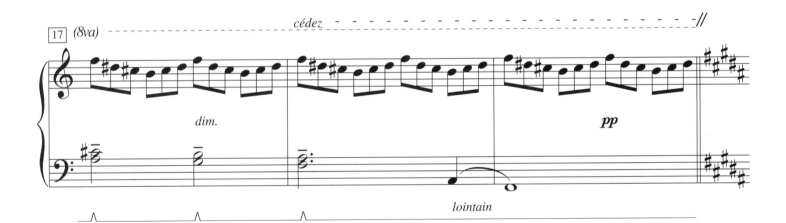

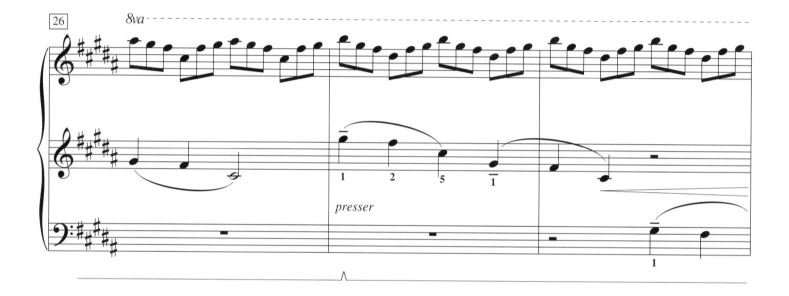

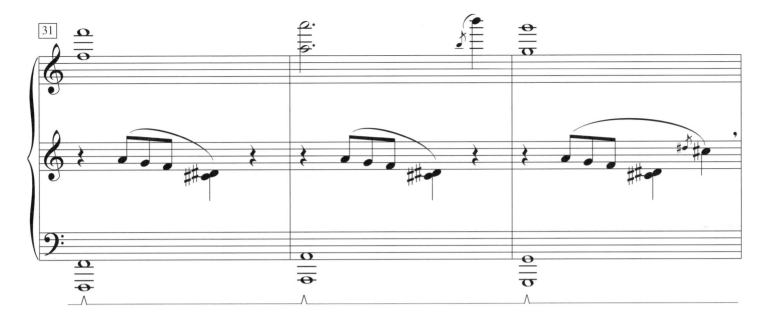

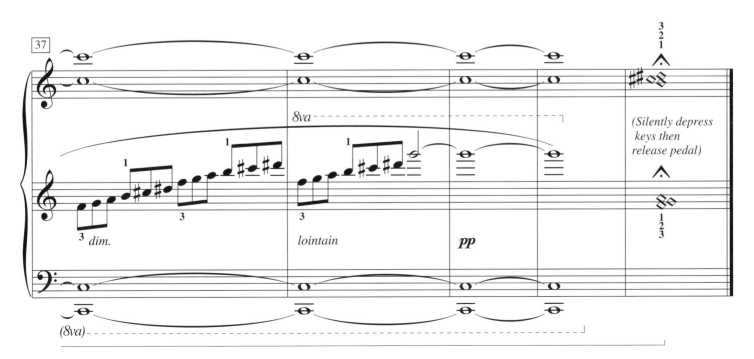

Northwoods Toccata

By Carol Klose

Allegro (♩ = 152-168)

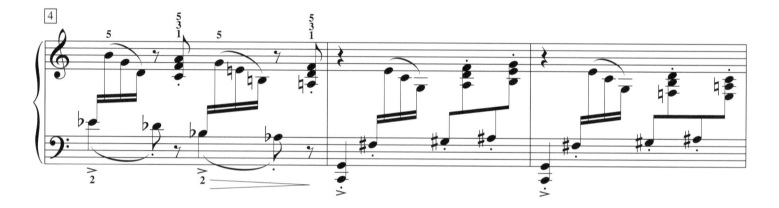

8va ⌐ ⌐
on repeat

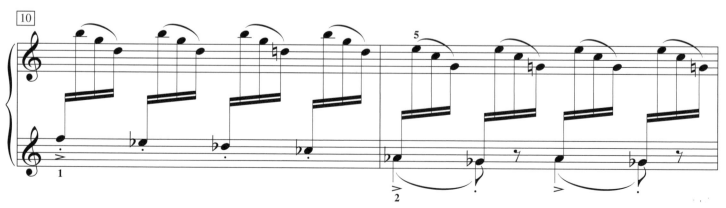

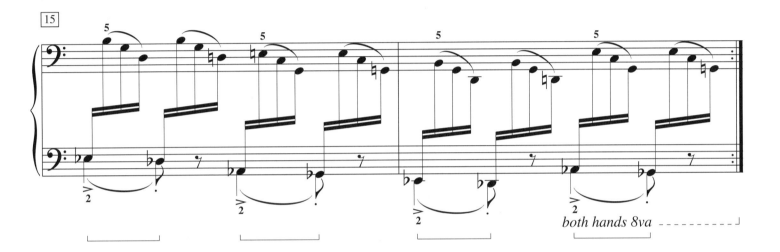

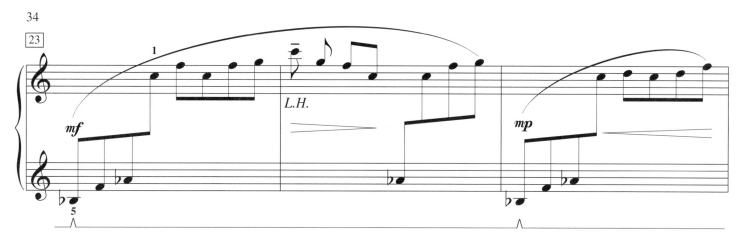

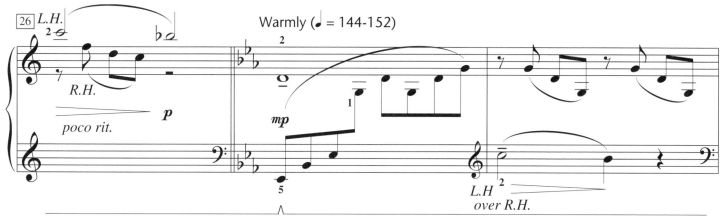

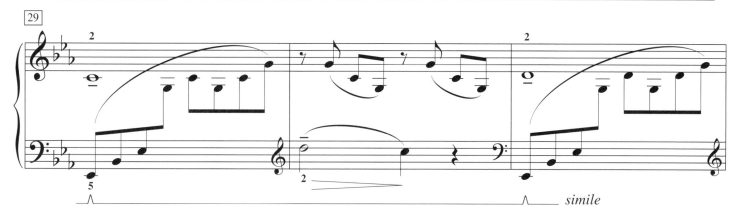

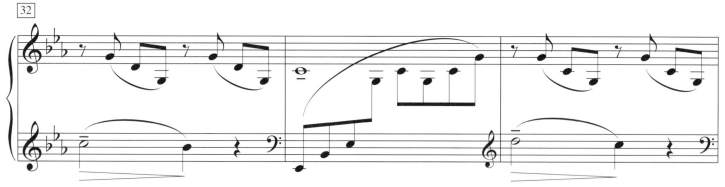

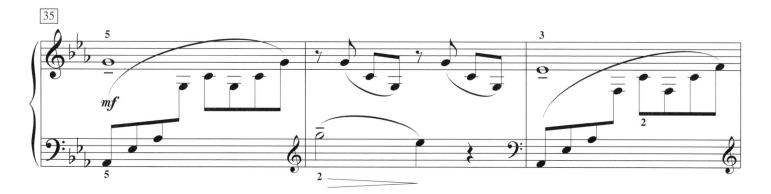

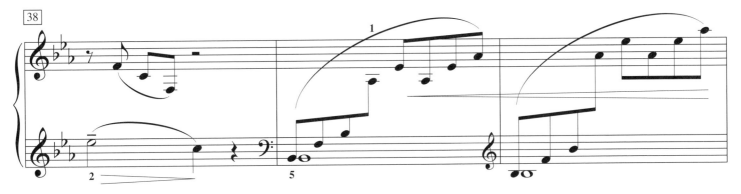

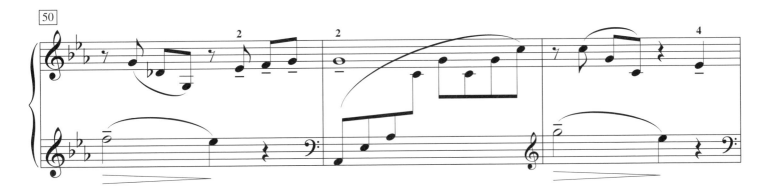

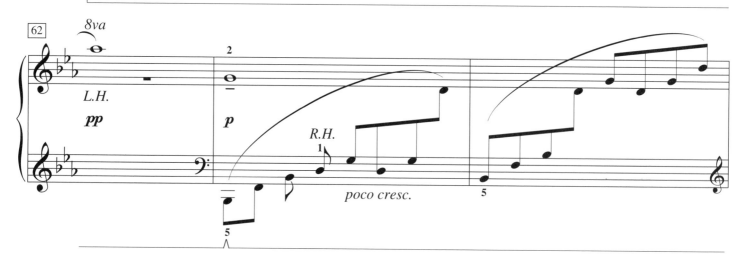

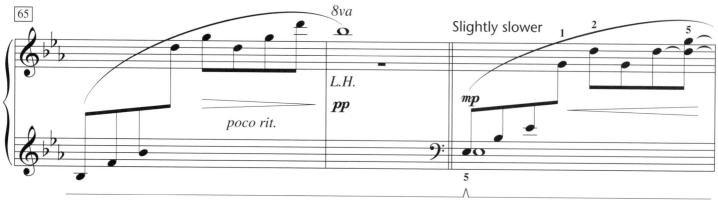

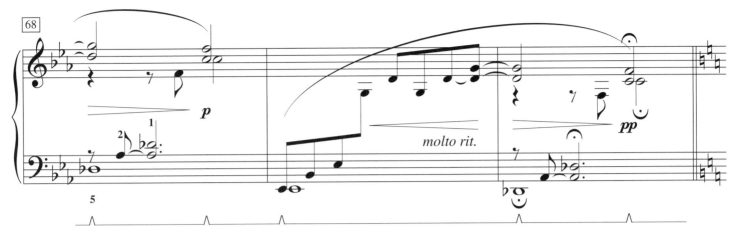

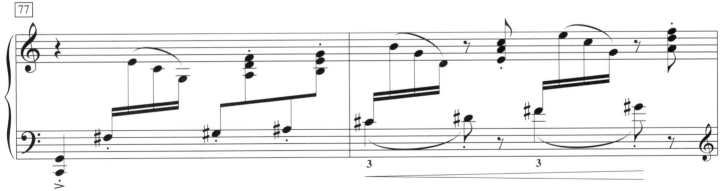

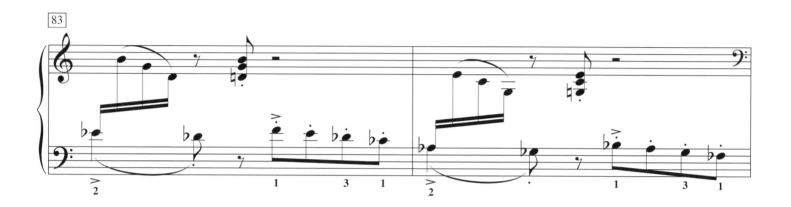

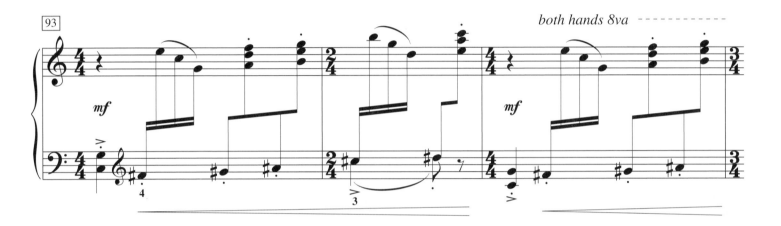

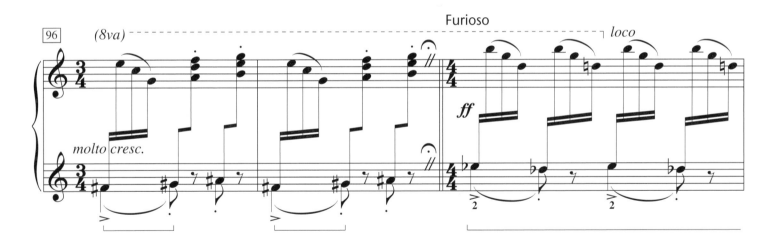

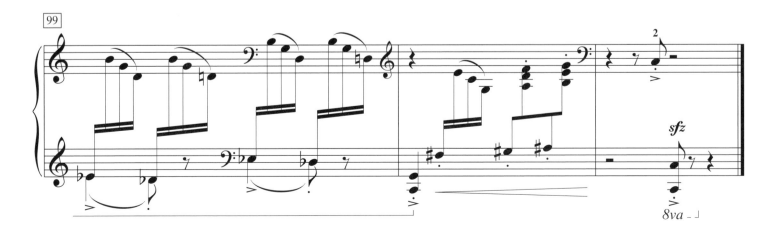

Sounds of the Rain

By Christos Tsitsaros

Moderato tranquillo (♩ = 104)

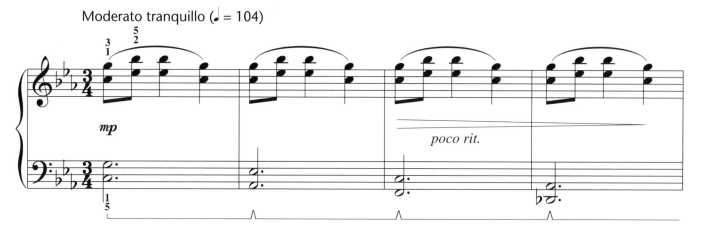

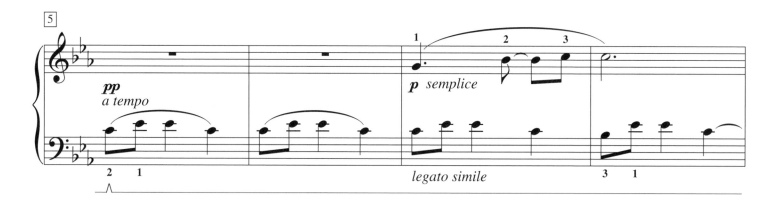

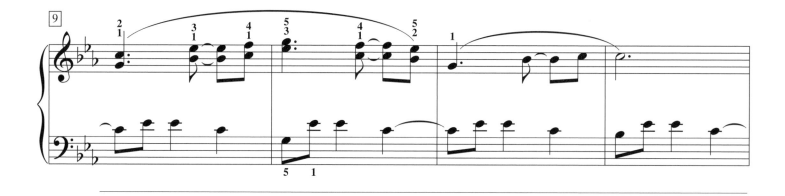

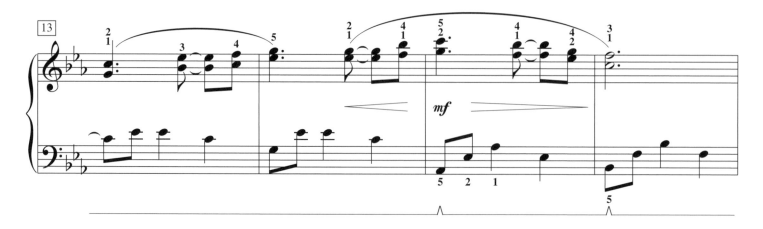

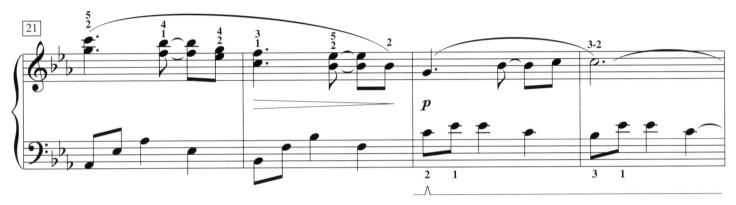

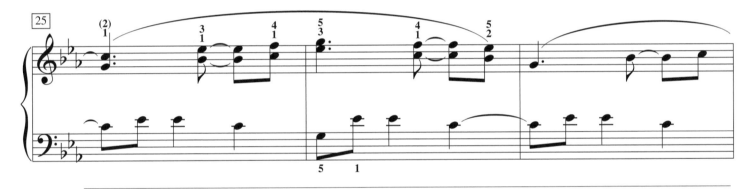

Poco più mosso e animato (♩ = 116-120)

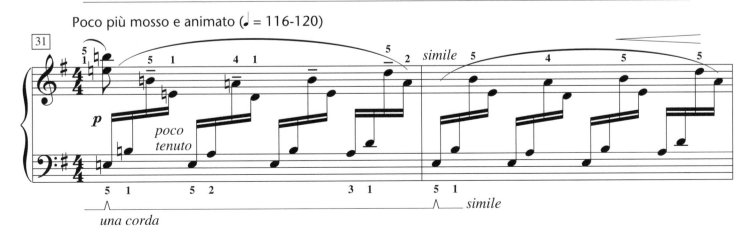

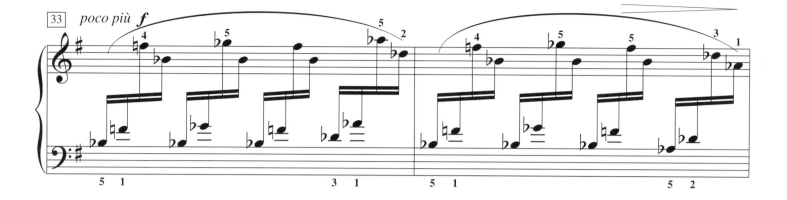

poco più **f**

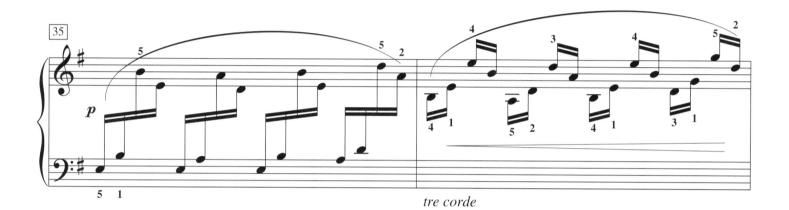

p

tre corde

mf

cresc.

sempre cresc. e accelerando

poco a poco dim. e calando*

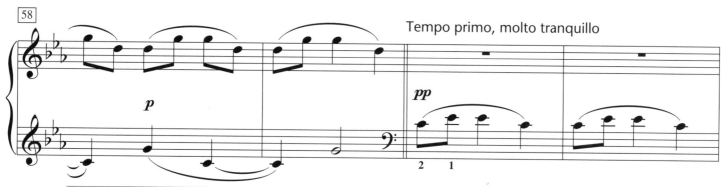

Tempo primo, molto tranquillo

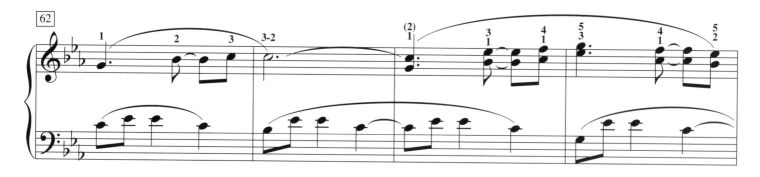

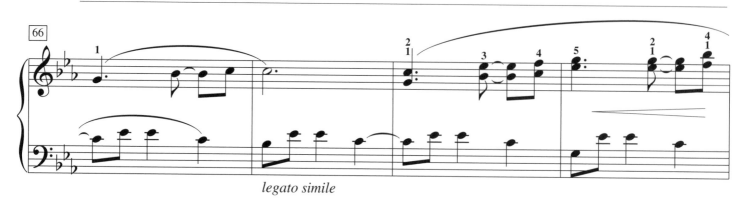

legato simile

*calando: dying away

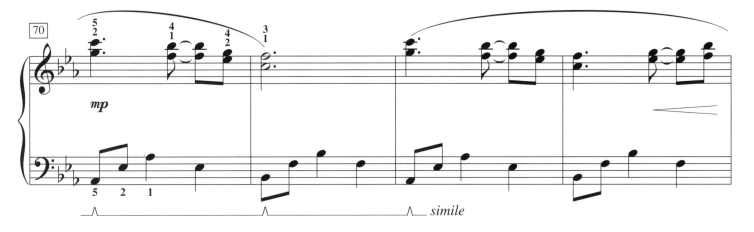

slentando: becoming slower

Jesters

By Christos Tsitsaros

Allegro animato (♩ = 108)

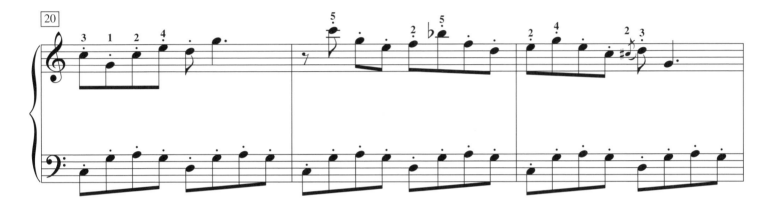

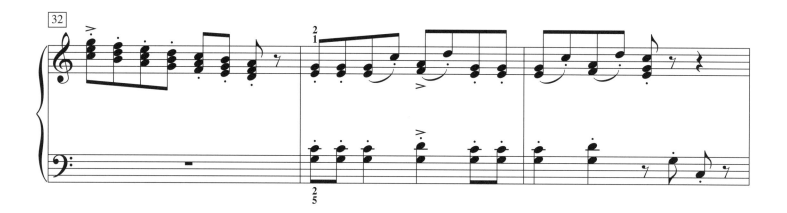

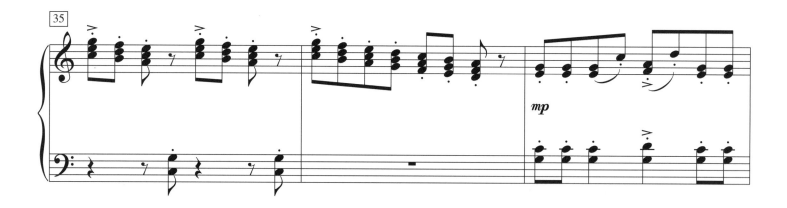

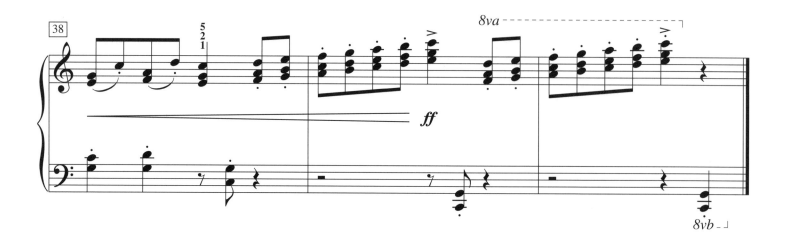